T0165093

The Most Beautiful
Gusu Fairy Tales

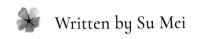 Written by Su Mei

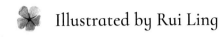 Illustrated by Rui Ling

The Old Cat Meiduo'er from the Sky

RC

Books Beyond Boundaries

ROYAL COLLINS

Interpreting Suzhou's Culture through Fairy Tale Picture Books

WANG QUANGEN

Chinese people are familiar with the saying, "Suzhou and Hangzhou are the heavens on earth."

Suzhou, a beautiful city with a rich culture of 2,500 years, has been an aesthetic inspiration throughout history. Still, depicting Suzhou's culture through illustrated fairy tales was unprecedented. Therefore, Soochow University Press invited Su Mei, a well-known local children's writer, and Rui Ling, an experienced illustrator, to co-create this book series. Aside from its pioneering role in this subject area, it is also the first "cultural picture book" series to combine Chinese elements, regional cultures, ethnic expressions, and fairy tale fantasies. For these reasons, I fell deeply in love with the books' words and images the moment I saw them.

Su Mei has a brilliant imagination and an exquisite style—she is a superb writer. Choosing a topic and putting it into words is a great challenge given Suzhou's colorful and diverse regional culture. Applying the method of time travel in fairy tale writing, Su Mei lets Meiduo'er, an old cat who has been away from Suzhou for a long time, fly back home out of concern for Tiancizhuang, which will soon be pulled down. With the help of a little girl, Nannan, she begins a journey to find her childhood friends ...

Through Meiduo'er's eyes, the author focused on elements that embody the most regional characteristics of Suzhou: river towns, gardens, Taihu Lake, embroidery, ginkgo trees, local snacks, the dialect, and silk. Each element is exemplified in a story; altogether, the stories connect Suzhou's regional cultures and customs effectively. By reading them, children can learn more about Suzhou.

Although the city's beauty is hard to delineate with lines and colors, illustrator Rui Ling did an excellent job in making the works vivid, engaging, and diverse.

I sincerely offer my congratulations on the publication of *The Most Beautiful Gusu Fairy Tales*. I hope that all children can benefit from Suzhou's splendid landscape and glorious culture.

WANG QUANGEN is a professor and doctoral advisor at the School of Chinese Language and Literature of Beijing Normal University, vice president of the Children's Literature Committee of the China Writers Association, and director of the China Children's Literature Education Research Center. He is also vice president of the Asia Children's Literature Research Academy, deputy director of the Professional Committee of Chinese Language Teaching in Chinese Contemporary Literature Research, and review expert of The National Social Science Fund of China. As a distinguished academic, he enjoys a special government allowance for life.

About the Writer:

SU MEI is a member of the China Writers Association and director of the China Society for the Studies of Children's Literature. She now teaches at Soochow University. Su has published over six hundred fairy tales and more than sixty story collections. Her math and science fairy tale picture books have been exported to Singapore, Malaysia, Thailand, Indonesia, and other countries. Many of her works have been selected for Chinese textbooks for kindergartens and US elementary schools. Su is the winner of many awards, including the "Second China Children's Book Gold Award," "Bing Xin Children's Literature Award," "Bing Xin Children's Book Award," and second place in the "First Sina Flash Fairy Tale Competition."

About the Illustrator:

ZHANG RUILING is a professional illustrator and picture book painter. Born in Heze, Shandong Province, Zhang studied at the Department of Design at Shandong College of Art and the Department of Photography at Beijing Film Academy. Her published works include *I Have a Date with Zhuangzi*, etc. Zhang was the winner of the "2012 Bing Xin Children's Book Award."

One morning, Meiduo'er, an old cat, woke up, and she pondered the dream she just had. In it, she saw her old childhood friend, Awang.

She has been
dreaming about him
and their young days
together quite a lot
lately. "I'm really
aging now," she
thought to herself.
"I'm getting so
nostalgic…"

She had her breakfast and sat down with today's newspaper. Suddenly, an article struck her like lightning: the Tiancizhuang area of Shizi Street in Suzhou will be torn down and rebuilt!

She put down the paper as her childhood memory rushed back to her again.

Back then, Meiduo'er was living in a house with a little garden in Tiancizhuang with Dr. Su and his family. Her best friend was Awang, a puppy.

Some time later, Dr. Su sold the house and moved to Beijing for his job. Meiduo'er moved with him, but Awang was left behind.

"I need to go back!" decided Meiduo'er. She pulled out a small suitcase under the bed and took out an embroidered carpet—a magical flying carpet! It needed some mending now because it was damaged during one flight over a mountain peak.

Her nanny, Auntie Ding, bought her gold and silver threads for the needlework.

From this day on, Meiduo'er forgot about eating and sleeping. She spent almost all her time mending the carpet.

After a week, she grew a lot thinner but much happier, because she finally fixed the carpet!

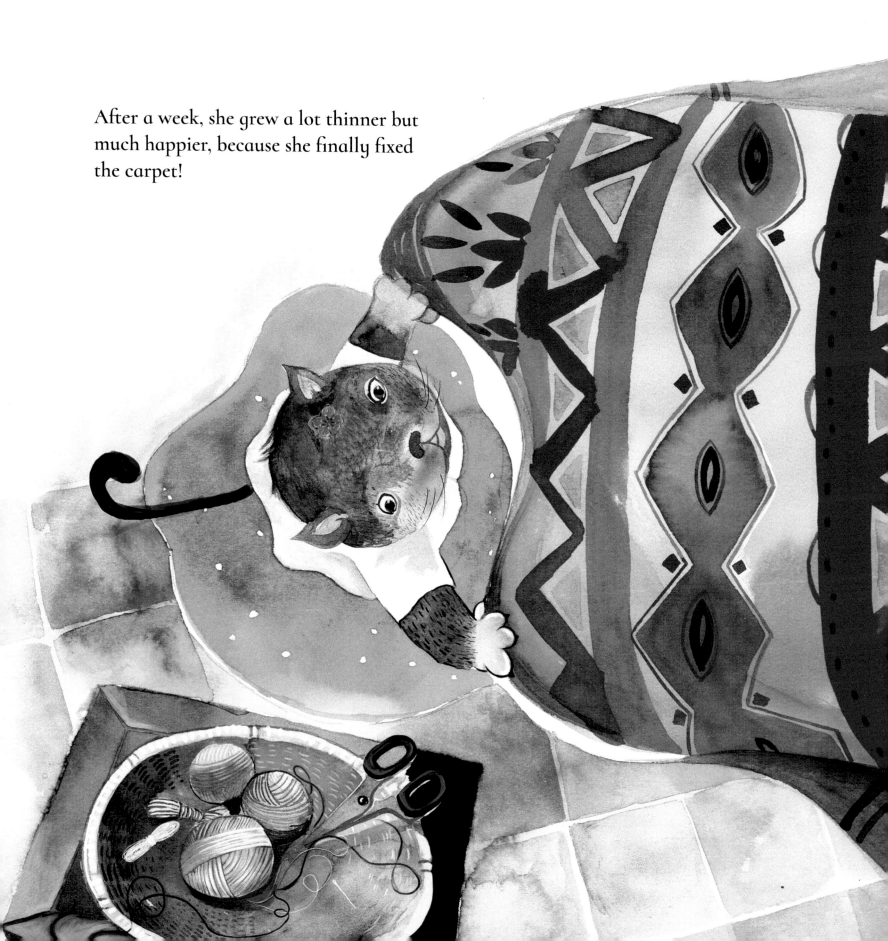

On a warm morning, Meiduo'er packed her luggage, left Dr. Su a letter, and set off on the flying carpet.

"Lock the gold and silver locks, unfold the gold and silver carpets. Avoid the mountains, away from the eagles, to the Tiancizhuang in Suzhou."

With the spell, the carpet flew up and took Meiduo'er to the south.

Before long, Meiduo'er arrived at Suzhou, at the dear little house she had been longing for days and nights. Meiduo'er was so excited!

A little girl saw her descending from the sky and asked in surprise, "Are you from heaven? I've always wished to have a magical cat like you!"

"My name is Meiduo'er, and I used to live here when I was young. I came back to find my childhood friend, Awang. He is a brave, kind, and naughty dog."

"Nannan, who are you talking to?"
someone asked from the house.

"Granny, I have a new friend, Meiduo'er. She lived here before."

"That's wonderful! Please invite your new friend in. I'll prepare her a bed."

Meiduo'er walked into her old room,
which was the little girl's room now.

"Can you please put my bed here?"
she asked.

"Of course." Nannan and her granny
helped her settle in.

Meiduo'er was tired and slept early that day.
She slept soundly, as if she had never left.

Nannan slept soundly, too, because she now had a friend from her dreams.

The next day after breakfast, Meiduo'er and Nannan went for a walk to the Wangxing Bridge. Many people lived here along the river.

The river was clear, and the flowers on the trees along the bank and in people's gardens were blooming.

Meiduo'er squinted in the sun and enjoyed the fragrant air. "They say Suzhou and Hangzhou are like paradise on earth. I think Suzhou in spring is even more beautiful than heaven!"

They strolled along the river and counted the little bridges that frequently appeared.

At Shouxing Bridge, they played a game of chasing each other from one side to the other again and again, laughing all the way.

"This was how Awang and I used to do it when we were young!" said Meiduo'er.

Just then, a little yellow dog ran toward them. Meiduo'er almost cried out, because he looked exactly like Awang when he was young!

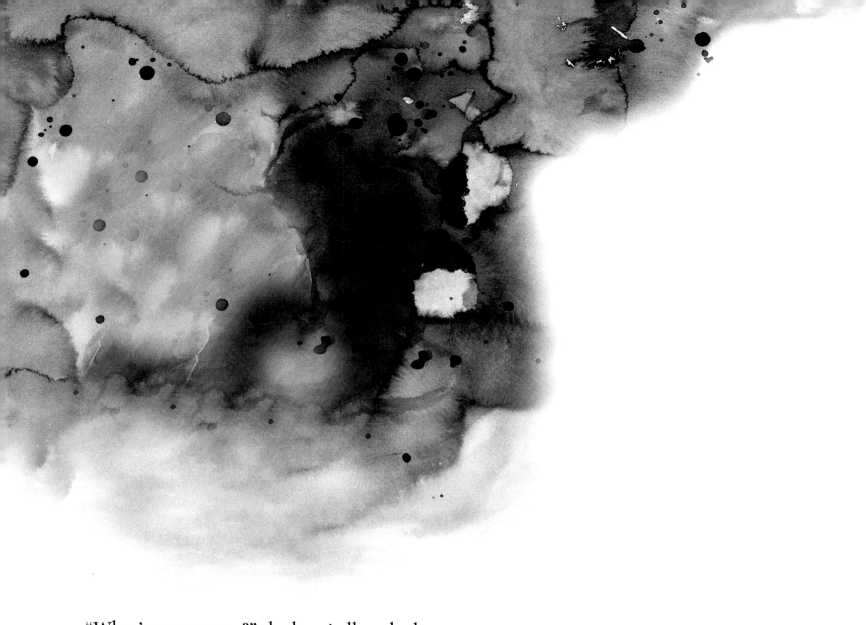

"What's your name?" she hurriedly asked.

"I'm San Wangzi." The puppy answered with a smile.
San Wangzi? What a strange name!

"Who's your father?" Meiduo'er asked again.

San Wangzi's smile disappeared. "He left two years ago,"
he said quietly. "People called him Yiquan."

Yiquan? Why do they all have such strange names?

San Wangzi ran away.

Meiduo'er watched him and said, "What a lovely, naughty little one! I really like him."

Knowledge
Station

As the saying goes, "There is heaven above, and there are Suzhou and Hangzhou below." Suzhou is an ancient city with 2,500 years of history in the Jiangnan (south of the Yangtze River) region. It is known for its rich culture, outstanding characters, and beautiful scenery.

🍃 The original bridge pier of Wangxing Bridge (Tiancizhuang)

🍃 Wangxing Bridge (Tiancizhuang)

🍃 The Wangxing Bridge today (Tiancizhuang)

Shouxing Bridge (Tiancizhuang)

The bridge floor of Shouxing Bridge (Tiancizhuang)

Shouxing Bridge (Tiancizhuang)

There are many bridges in the ancient city of Suzhou, with more than 25 bridges every square kilometer in its most densely distributed area. There are 314 bridges painted in the *Map of Pingjiang* (now Suzhou) in the Song Dynasty (960–1279), 300 marked in the *General Map of Waterways in Suzhou* in the Ming Dynasty (1368–1644), 311 painted in the *Map of Suzhou City* in the Qing Dynasty (1616–1912), and 361 recorded in the *Annals of Suzhou City* in 1985.

The Tang poet Bai Juyi once said, "Green waves on four sides, red bridges three hundred and ninety."

Du Xunhe, a contemporary poet, also said, "If you go to Gusu, you'll see everyone lives by the river. In this ancient, crowded city, there is little free land but many small rivers and bridges."

🌿 Sipo Bridge (Pingjiang Street)

🌿 The stone civet cat at the head of the bridge (Shantang Street)

Suzhou is also known as the "Venice of the East" and "Water City of the East."

🌸 Leading to Quietude Bridge (Master of the Nets Garden)

🌸 Wannian Bridge (Moat)

Nannan's Ancient Poems

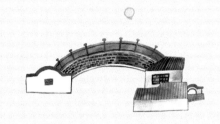

Docked at Maple Bridge Overnight

by Zhang Ji

The setting Moon, the raven's caw, frost-filled skies,

River maples, fishing lights, sleep of eternal darkness.

Outside of Gusu City and Hanshan Temple,

Midnight tolls, the passenger boat arrives ...

Docking at Gusu

by Wang Anshi (1021–1086)

At dawn, wandering to Panmen in the east;

At dusk, leaving Changmen in the west.

I see no one around me, only the sun, pale and setting.

The twilight mist covers the trees and the home-coming birds.

They have a home to return to, but I am all alone.

Dreaming of the Southern Shore

by Bai Juyi (772–846)

Fair Jiangnan,

An old familiar scene,

Sunrise riverside fire-red flowers,

Spring river sapphire-blue waves,

How can I forget Jiangnan?

Seeing a Friend Off to Wu

by Du Xunhe (846–904)

Seeing you off to Gusu.

At home there, all are sleeping by the stream.

An ancient palace with few unattended plots.

By the harbor, many small bridges.

In the night market, water chestnuts.

Spring barges bring satins and gauze.

Knowing that far away, the moon still watches.

Think of me there, in the fisherman's song.

The Most Beautiful Gusu Fairy Tales:
The Old Cat Meiduo'er from the Sky

Written by Su Mei
Illustrated by Rui Ling
Translated by Wu Meilian

First published in 2024 by Royal Collins Publishing Group Inc.
Groupe Publication Royal Collins Inc.
BKM Royalcollins Publishers Private Limited

Headquarters: 550-555 boul. René-Lévesque O Montréal (Québec)
H2Z1B1 Canada
India office: 805 Hemkunt House, 8th Floor, Rajendra Place, New
Delhi 110 008

Original Edition @ Soochow University Press

ISBN: 978-1-4878-1185-3

To find out more about our publications,
please visit www.royalcollins.com.